Black Coffee:
Poems to Get African American Women through the Day

Thomalyn A. Epps

authorHOUSE®

AuthorHouse™
1663 Liberty Drive, Suite 200
Bloomington, IN 47403
www.authorhouse.com
Phone: 1-800-839-8640

First published by AuthorHouse 4/6/2009

ISBN: 978-1-4389-6801-8 (sc)

Printed in the United States of America
Bloomington, Indiana

This book is printed on acid-free paper.

Black Coffee

A cup of black coffee
To warm the spirit
Pick you up
At the beginning of the day
Fill up your soul
Give you the energy
To keep on fighting
For one more day
This world is tough
Especially on us
And sometimes we need
A little Black Coffee
To perk us up!

Dedicated to: My Mother

Contents

I. Black Women

Ten Commandments for Black Women

1. Thou shall not succumb to envy
We should be happy to see our sisters succeed.

2. Thou shall not depend on a man
A man we may want but we should not need.

3. Thou shall love every inch of thou shape
Whether size 2 or size 10, every inch of us is great.

4. Thou shall help another sister when you can
If we all work together, taller we will stand.

5. Thou shall appreciate thou unique beauty
The beauty God gave us which everyone can see.

6. Thou shall always take care of thou children
They are your fruit, the responsibility you were given.

7. Thou shall always take care of yourself
For both your physical and emotional health.

8. Thou shall always respect your body
It is your temple, hold it up highly.

9. Thou shall live by God's word
The words from the Bible should be the loudest heard.

10. Thou shall make sure you have some fun
It's your life and you are only given one.

Black Beauty

Black Beauty

Black girl you have a beauty that shines
   Bright as the sun
A unique look which makes you
   The envy of everyone

From café au lait
   To black coffee no cream
To touch your beautiful black skin
   Is every man's dream

With your curvy hips
   And well defined thighs
You are better than a size five
   In any man's eyes

Naturally thick lips,
   No need for injection
The expensive desire
   Of many other women

Thick kinky hair
   And deep brown eyes
When your eyes light up
   It's like a sunrise

Black girl you are beautiful
   Outside and in
A heavenly beauty
   To be worshipped by men.

The Beauty Within

Having outer beauty is nice
A pretty face
Long beautiful hair
A body to make men drool
But, if that's all you have
I feel sorry for you
You don't have real beauty
A beauty that is true;
The world might see the outside first
But what happens
When people start to look in
If your inside is ugly
That will show through
And your pretty face
Will only matter to you
Are you a good person
You need to ask yourself
For this is far more important in the end
Do you have a good heart
To match your pretty face
A beautiful soul
To match your outer grace?

Mirror, Mirror

Mirror mirror on the wall
Who is the finest of them all?
With all her style
And all her grace
And her beautiful brown ebony face
Doe brown eyes
And thick brown nose
Beautiful from her head to her toes
Stately lips
And shapely hips
She holds the world at her fingertips
Mirror mirror on the wall
Who is the queen of them all?

Beautiful

You look at me
And you don't see
The beauty that I am
The outside package
May be right you see
But that is not
My real beauty;
You can't see my heart
Or look at my soul
But those are beautiful things
You should really get to know
My heart and my mind
May not be obvious
But those are the places
I really shine
I am more special
Than you could ever see
If you just take a second
To look at me
Listen to me speak
Hear my ideas
Get to know my thoughts
Get to know my fears
Because my true beauty
Resides inside me
It is not something
Your eye can see.

Brown Eyes

Beautiful brown eyes
Deep and full of expression
Warm and glowing
The eyes of a black woman
These eyes have seen a lot
And absorbed it all
Still brown and beautiful
The eyes of our soul.

The Strength of a Black Woman

The Soul of a Black Woman

The soul of a black woman
Is fierce and strong
And proud of who she is
She knows where she's going
And where she came from
Never forgetting her heritage;
The soul of a black woman
Is rich and pure
And filled with lots of love
For her family and her community;
The soul of a black woman
Is full of faith
She knows God gave her this day
And in times when she needs Him
She'll get on her knees and pray;
The soul of a black woman
Is very resilient
If she falls she will get back up
She know that she has to keep on striving
Even if she gets down on her luck;
The soul of a black woman
Is very unique
There is no one like her
She possesses distinct qualities
Characteristics of a Nubian queen
Are in each and every one of us.

Strength

I know I am strong
Because I am still here
Still standing
In spite of my fear
Not hindered by those
Who try to hold me back
I am a strong black woman
And I know that
I can weather the storm
And make it through
No breaking in the wind
Even when others do
This black woman
Will always stand tall
Fighting and surviving
I will never fall
Because I know
I might not have everything
But one thing I do have
Is infinite strength.

Hold On

Hold on when bad times are all around
Hold on when life has got you down
Hold on when you can't seem to find a friend
Hold on knowing that on Jesus you can depend;
Hold on when your job is lost
Hold on when you can't seem to afford what anything costs
Hold on when the pain seems too much to bare
Hold on when life seems to be a nightmare
Hold on when you look in the mirror and don't like what you see
Hold on in time knowing what you can be;
Hold on when you are wondering what the future holds
Hold on through all of life's trying woes
Hold on when life get too tough
Hold on even when you think you've had enough;
Grab onto something and hold on tight
To make it through the darkest night
Hold on for dawn will finally come
And a new day is waiting just over the horizon.

The Power of a Black Woman

A black woman has the power
To make a black man weak
Forget all his thoughts
Make him the only thing he sees;
She can hook him
With only a smile
He'll turn his back on his friends
At least for a little while;
A black woman has the power
To support a black man
Be his strong backbone
Encourage him to be all he can
She also has the power
To understand his plight
All he is going through
She is fighting the same fight;
A black woman has the power
To give a black man true love
A heavenly love
Sent from God above
A black woman has the power
To do many things
That black woman has the power
To make him a black king.

What it Means to be a Black Woman

What Does Being a Black Woman Really Mean

Does being a black woman mean
    being a rock
Being a strong woman
    around the clock
Does being black woman mean
    putting people in check
Schooling anyone
    who tries to disrespect
Does being a black woman mean
    standing by a black man
A man who is not doing anything
    and doesn't have a plan
Does being a black woman mean
    disliking a white
Not giving her a chance
    because she doesn't understand our fight
Does being a black woman mean
    talking in slang
Sounding as if
    school didn't teach us a thing
No being a black woman
    is none of this
These stereotypical images
    we don't have to fit
Being a black woman means
    being you
And remembering where you come from
    in all that you do
Being a black woman
    is who you are
A beautiful black shining star.

Black Enough

I ask you to tell me
Who is the judge
The judge of my blackness
My spirit, my identity
How black am I
As black as you
Is your culture stronger
Because of what you've been through
A suburban girl
You question my roots
Saying I'm not down
Because I'm not like you
When I speak you make fun
My English is too clean
And some things I enjoy
Are not 'black' things
Does this mean I'm not ebony
A Nubian queen
My blackness I don't question
So who are you
The standard of blackness
The acceptable mold
My skin is chocolate brown
And my heritage is gold.

Token

I represent all black women
As soon as I open my mouth
An entire race of people
Is judged by my every action
I can't just go through life
Thinking only of me
I have to make sure I represent
Black women positively;
I have a tremendous weight
I carry everyday
Never getting a change to slip up
Cut loose, not worry about it
Although it may not be fair to me
To carry this burden along
I know I am not the only one
So I continue to be strong
Make sure I represent us well
In everything I do
Because I know that my actions
Will reflect on you.

I Am the Only

I am the only one
Who can be me
A beautiful black queen
But very unique
To embrace the difference
I have from others
And would never change
To be like another;
I am the only one
Who sees the world
Through my eyes
My viewpoint is special
Because it's only mine
The way I look at things
May not be like them
But I know
I'm not the same
As other women;
I am the only one
Who really knows me
When others look at me
They might not see the same thing
But I know who I am
And to myself I'll be true
I'll be me
And let you be you.

II. The Black Man

Words of Praise

Black King

Deep ebony eyes
Thick ebony nose
His beauty is something only heaven knows

His big strong hands
And muscular thighs
His smile is like sunshine

His chocolate brown skin
Dreds, bald, or cornrows
His spirit is so mighty it glows

A deep base in his voice
A cool pimp in his walk
The uniquely expressive way only he can talk

Whether baggy jeans and hoodies
Business suits or blue collar
He works hard and knows the value of a dollar

Black African King
Sitting on his ebony throne
Every black queen would love to have him as her own.

Sexy

Brother you are the epitome of sexy
In everything you do
The confidence you radiate
The attention you command
Whenever you enter a room
Your slick black skin
Your beautiful brown eyes
I love everything about you
Your walk is mean
And the way you talk
You know you're a sexy thing
The pride you have
The clothes you wear
The way you never let anyone knock you down
Sexy is your lightening smile
You don't just shine you glean
Brother you are a sexy specimen
Of masculine perfection
Your personality, your soul
Your style, your flare
Sexier than you'll ever know.

Message to Black Men

Ladies Night

The girls are coming over
No men are allowed
We are going to party tonight
Go out with the crowd;
You hang with your boys
Every Friday night
So why should I just sit at home
That isn't right;
I'm going to put on my best dress
And fix up my hair
Throw on some make-up
To make all the men stop and stare
Don't ask me where I'm going
Why do you need to know
Just know that I'll have fun tonight
Where ever I may go
See I have resolved
Not to sit around and wait for you
So for one night I'll go clubbing
And forget about you
Don't try to stop me
I don't want to fight
You're going to make me late
Tonight is ladies' night out.

Better Than Ten

I am better than ten women
Who want a man for his cash
Looking for someone to take care of them
Instead of supporting themselves;
I am better than any woman
Who would trade sex for his loot
Because even if she's not walking the street
She is still a prostitute;
I am better than ten women
Who judge a man by his car
Heading to the club every weekend
Hoping to hook up with a star;
I am better than ten women
Who are using a man to get
Everything they want in life
But aren't willing to work for it;
But Brothers you seem to go for them
Because they give you what you like
Then lump us all in the same category
Saying all sisters just aren't right
Well, maybe you should raise your standards
Above those scandalous women
Because I may be just one woman
But I am better than ten of them.

Interracial Dating

Why Is He With Her?

Is it the straight blonde hair no need for relaxer,
Which has you so eager to hold her hand?
Or is it her milky white skin
Which has her in such high demand
You have stopped admiring pretty brown eyes
Now you seem to prefer them blue
My girls and I sit around talking for hours
About what in the world is wrong with you
Is it that she was the forbidden fruit
The plantation master tried to keep you away from for so long
That makes you so proud to walk around
Parading her on your arm
Is she supposed to be your status symbol
To show you finally have arrived
Or is she your ticket into the "club"
To make them finally accept you
Or maybe she is the perfect size 6
Like a Cosmo cover model
What is it? Please tell me, I want to know
What is she your chosen queen?
Is it that my nose is too thick
And you like them straight and button small
I know its not that my lips are too big
Because she would pay to have them too
I know I'm not the standard of beauty in the white man's eyes
But it seems like you have his eyes now too
All I ask is brother why?
What is it about her that makes her appeal to you
Is it the way she talks,
Only the kings English touches her lips
Or is it that she is soft spoken,

And never talks back to you
Do you think I'm too mean, too lazy, too overweight?
Is that why you never look my way anymore
Preferring to turn to her
To treasure and adore
After years and years of having your back
I feel like you have turned on me
Why do you prefer to be with her
Over your beautiful black queen?

Should I Stick To Brothers

When I see you walk around
With a blonde by your side
I wonder why I am so loyal to you
Not giving other men a chance
Should I stick to brothers
Or shop around
Explore other men the way you do
What about an Asian love
Could he be as good as you
Many Caucasian men are kind of cute
Maybe I'll give them a chance, too
Or a Spanish man, Frenchman,
Try something new
Broaden my horizons
There are so many options
Instead of sitting here waiting for you.

Comments

Who Is the Man

Is the man the one
   who has the most cash
But is always to busy working
   to show his woman love;
Is the man the one
   who is built like a god
With a chiseled face
   sent from heaven above;
Is the man the one
   with all the degrees
And an arrogant attitude
   to match his PhD;
There are many men out there
   who think they're the man
Can you spot the man
   know who he might be;
Is the man the one
   who can get plenty of women
With whom he can spend
   a lot of his time
The pimp, player,
   the ladies man
One who knows
   how to wine and dine;
Or is the man
   the center of attention
The one who knows
   how to entertain
The popular man
   with plenty of friends
And everybody around him
   knows his name
How about the man

with the most kids
And a number of women
   in whom he planted his seed
Does being a baby's daddy
   make him the man
Even if he doesn't do for his kids
   all that he can
There are plenty of men
   with lots of clout
But do they have what it takes to be the man
   this I really doubt;
The man is the one
   who cherishes love
And for his family he will sacrifice
   that's what a real man is made of
The man will never
   put his hands on you
And to you he will always
   be faithful and true
So if you are wondering
   who really is the man
You have to look inside
   see his heart if you can
Because though he may not
   get the most attention
He will be a good man
   who loves his woman.

A Good Woman

Do you know a good woman
When you see one
Or are your only qualifications
Pretty and young;
Do you take the time
To get to know what she's about
Or do you ignore her inside
And focus on what's out;
A good woman may not be
The beauty queen
But she is better than even
The most beautiful lady
Because she knows
How to treat her man
And she has a big heart
To give you all the love she can;
But many men seem
To look for the wrong things
And then wonder why
Their woman is not what they dreamed;
Their superficial eyes
Finds a superficial heart
A lady who was
No good from the start;
But if he looked for a good woman
He surely would find
That in the end
She is the real dime.

Create A Man

If I could create
The perfect man
Make him everything
I want him to be
I would first
Give him a heart
And the eyes of his heart
Would look only to me;
Next I would teach him
A little respect
Not just for me
But for himself
To be good to him
And to be good to me
That man has to
Think of himself highly;
After respect
I would give him courage
Because in this world
He has to stand up for himself
Not letting others push him around
Because others will surely
Try to knock him down
But I wouldn't always
Want him to be strong
He would need to know
The meaning of compassion
And sensitivity is a quality
This man would need
So he could be there for me
When I am feeling weak;
I would make him an educated man
A man with some drive
To work as hard as he can
And then I would throw in

A little something for me
I would make sure I sculpt
The perfect body
With skin so smooth
And chocolate brown
A man who can dress
When we go out on the town
I know this may be
A lot for one man
But I will create
This man if I can.

Low Down

As a woman I have often worried
That my man may cheat on me
Questioning in the back of my mind
Whether he is with another lady
But in this day and age
Maybe a lady's not all I should fear
Our men have somehow become attracted
To another brother's rear
And these relationships are far more dangerous
Than the one they have with women
The chaos that is being created
Is fueling an epidemic
Our beautiful brothers are now engaging
In acts which put us at risk
Poisoning their women by their actions
Without even thinking about it
Ladies we need to stop relying
On our man to keep us safe
What is plaguing our community
Is endangering our whole race
Start taking steps to keep your own self safe
Proactive in protecting your health
Don't blindly trust him with your life
Think about yourself
Many brothers won't admit
The things they do in the dark
But if you are not careful sisters
He may do more than break your heart
Why some brothers are turning to each other
I really don't know
But can I spot him when I see him
I just don't think so
He looks like any other brother
The men you see everyday
Never wanting to show a sign

To anyone he might be gay
So now I think the time has come
When all men are suspect
So I will keep my eyes open
Knowing not all brothers are what I expect.

Where Is My Man

Where is love
When you're all alone;
Why can't you find it
When you need it most;
It feels like I have my heart in my hand
But I can't seem to find the right man
Someone who'll be everything I need
A man willing to be there for me
Someone by my side through thick and thin
Where on earth is this man hiding?
Where is my man
Where could he be
Looking everywhere for someone for me
Traveled many thousand miles from home
But I'm still sitting here all alone
I need someone I can hold onto
I don't want to walk this road alone
So I'm still waiting for the day
When he will come and give my heart a home;
I'm a good woman
With so much to give
No not perfect but then who is?
I can be everything that he wants me to be
If he would just reveal himself to me
All I need is someone to love
Some quality time and some affection
What is it, are all the good men are taken?
But I know there's gotta be one left
Where, where, where is he?
Without love this world sometimes gets lonely
I just want a little of his company
Not asking for all of his time
I just want to hold him for a little while

Where is my man?
Where could he be?
I'm looking everywhere for someone for me.

III. Love

First Love

Speechless

I knew I loved him before I met him
With a love so deep it filled my soul
I walk his way just to see him
But shy away before approach
I watch him as he passes by
Studying his every move
Admiring my cutie from a distance
Hoping to one day build up the nerve to get closer
Everyday I wait for him
Trying to appear nonchalant
But as he gets nearer I can feel the heat rising in my face
Knowing I must be red as a beet
I want to turn and run
But then he says hello
And I just stand there
Speechless.

Unknown Love

Mystery Woman

You don't know me
But you should want to
Because I am the one
Who wants you
To take care of you
And treat you like a king
To be there for you
Be your everything;
But you haven't noticed
Never bothered to ask my name
Choosing to entertain other women
Girls who aren't genuine;
I would be better for you
Than any one of those
I would be better for you
Than anyone you chose
But I can't even seem
To catch a glimpse for your eye
Make you look my way
No matter how hard I try
But, I will still keep trying
To get to know you
Hoping that one day
You will want to know me too.

Looking for Love

Looking for Love

When you go looking for love
It is hard to find
It hides away where you can't see
The more you look
The more love quivers
Ducking further from your eyes;
Love can feel you looking for it
So love begins to wear a disguise
Mr. Right Here starts to look like love
And Mr. Right Now can fool you too
Mr. You Can Do Better starts to seem so promising
With a little work he'll surely do;
All the while love is still hiding
Evading the glance of your prying eyes
See, love is shy, a little timid
It will only come out of hiding on its own time
So stop looking for love
Or you will scare it
And from you it will continue to hide
Just be patient and wait on love
And your heart, love will soon find.

Mr. Right

Who is my Mr. Right you ask
Where is he and why can't I find him
When I meet him how will I know;
If you look with your heart
Maybe you'll see him
But if you close your heart to him
You'll let him go
See Mr. Right may not be Mr. Handsome
And he probably isn't Mr. Rich
Mr. Right maybe not be smooth and cool
Big man on campus, king of the school
Mr. Right may not wear a suit
He may wear work boots instead of wingtip shoes
Mr. Right may not be six-six
He may even look up to you
But Mr. Right will make you feel good
Like you're the finest girl around
Mr. Right will make you laugh;
Around Mr. Right you can let your hair down
Mr. Right might not impress your friends
But you'll be impressed by the way he treats you
Though he might not have a lot of material things
He will fulfill all your emotional needs
So girl if you really want to find your Mr. Right
Look for the things that really matter
Look with your heart open for Mr. Right
And your Mr. Right will soon appear.

All The Good Ones Are Taken

Every time I see a brother
  with his stuff together
He is always in a relationship
  taken by another
And oftentimes I feel as if
  these ladies aren't up to par
But no matter how I feel about it
  in his life she's the star
They say all the successful ones
  are ugly, married, or gay
Well maybe I take the ugly one
  give him a little play
But most of the brothers I come across
  aren't going anywhere
Instead of working hard for something
  its like they don't even care
They don't know how to treat a lady
  do a woman right
Where are all the good men hiding
  somewhere out of sight
All that I have are few requests
  I want a man to fill
I am not asking him to take care of me
  or pay a single bill
I just want a good loving man
  to whom I could give my heart
But to find a good man worthy of me
  I don't even know where to start.

Waiting

I am waiting for you
To come into my life
To come sweep me up
Take me away
Shower my heart
With tender love
I am waiting patiently
For that day
When you will appear
Right before me
I have dreamed of you
Molded your personality
I know just how you'll be
And now I sit
Waiting and waiting
Hoping you won't be
Too late.

Help Wanted

I've got a position
I need someone to fill
A vacancy in my heart
Searching for a suitable candidate
Someone who will work full-time
At building a relationship
This is not a temporary assignment
Therefore, you need not apply
If you can't make a commitment
No experience is necessary
However, you must be willing to learn
All that you need to know
To make our love strong
You must be available on-call
As love is a 24/7 job
And if you are wondering about compensation
You will be paid with true love
If you feel this is for you
I am taking applications
And the most suitable candidates
Will be granted a phone interview
To apply, please approach
And start a conversation
And I will soon get back to you
With my evaluation.

$In\,Love$

I Want To Love You

I want to love you
For everything you are
To know all about you
Get inside your head and heart
To know your thoughts and feelings
I want to be there for you
When you are feeling weak
I want to be your anchor
On a turbulent sea
I want to love you
If you will just give me the chance
I'll be everything you need
A raincoat to protect you from the storm
A security blanket to keep you warm
For you, I'll be all you're looking for
I want to love you
No one could love you more.

Real Love

Real love is not a fairy tale
Filled with countless moonlit strolls
Candlelight dinners and flowers everyday
And every night hot passionate love;
Real love is not perfect
Everyday won't be Valentine's Day
True love you have to work at;
Real love is not a fantasy
Love takes time and patience
And a lot of understanding
You give of yourself to someone else
In the good times and the bad
Stand by his side and hold him up
When he can't stand on his own;
Real love is not what movies are made of
But real love is everything.

Obsession

Wondering where you are
Every minute of the day
Not a moment in time
When you don't consume my thoughts
I can barely do my work
Can't barely concentrate
Missing you the moment
You start to walk away;
I can't wait for the day to be over
So I can rush right home to you
My friends say I have abandoned them
Because all I want is to be with you
I need to be in your arms
To feel your tender kiss
In the moments we are apart
It's those little things I miss
I think I love you
I think I am obsessed with you
You monopolize my heart and mind.

What It Means To Love Someone

Loving someone means accepting him
For the person that he is
In spite of all his flaws and faults
Taking the good with the bad
It's tough to truly love someone
To give him all your heart
To place yourself in a vulnerable position
That might tear your heart apart
But if you truly love someone
You are willing to take that chance
The chance that you may be hurt
By your love for that man;
And love is also a lot of work
It's not so easy to do
When you love someone
You have to think of him
Not just think about you
In love you often have to sacrifice
And do what's best for him
Give him the support to hold him up
When he needs a friend
See love is not an easy feeling
That you can quickly achieve
Many people throw around the word
Not knowing what loving someone really means.

Love Letter

I wanted to tell you
How special you are to me
You will always be
My beautiful black king
The love of my life
The rock I cling to
I am at my best
When I am with you;
You give me strength
Because you are strong
And I am there for you
If you need someone to lean on;
I love you more
With each passing day
And I will love you
For the rest of my days
You are the greatest man
I have ever known
And my love will always
Be yours alone.

I'll Be Your Rock

I'll be the rock
In the raging river of life
That never gets washed out to sea
Strong and stable is my love
And like a rock
I will never change
Imbedded in the river floor
I will stay right there
Something you can hold onto
Whenever reach for me.

Would You Still Love Him

Would you still love him
If he didn't have dime to his name
Instead of a Beamer
He drove a Hyundai
If he couldn't afford
The fancy places you like
Would you still be the woman
Standing by his side
And if he didn't
Have the washboard abs
And there was a little more to love;
Would he still be the man
You curl up to at night
Holding him close
And hugging him tight
And let's say he wasn't
A popular man
With plenty of friends
The center of attention
Would you still love him
Without the superficial things
Would you have taken his hand
And worn his ring
You say you love him
But ask yourself
Do you really love him
Is your love really true?

All I Need

I don't need
All of life's riches
A lot of material wealth
Tenuous insignificant things
Things that others have
The fancy cars
The expensive jewelry
Brand name labels
On my clothes
I don't care
About these things
The key to my heart
They do not hold;
All I need
Is one true love
To bring me happiness
His loving heart
And open arms
To me are everything;
Love is the greatest
Gift that someone
Could ever give to me
So he can keep his money
Fancy trip and trinkets
His love is
All I need.

Open Window

You snuck into my heart
Like a burglary in the night
Prying your way into my soul
Breaking in an open window
I didn't see it coming
Didn't want to fall in love
I had every intention
Of keeping you at a distance
Didn't want to let you in
But I forgot to put up my defenses
A closed heart with no lock
And somehow you managed
To find your way in
Found a vulnerable spot
I never did quite picture myself
With a man like you
But now I can't see me living
In this world without you.

Wedding Song

I want to be with you
Until the end of time
Be right beside you
Holding your hand in mine
Be the one to love you
In the good times and the bad
Always be there for you
In your arms forever;
I will always love you
No matter what life may bring
Be the lady in your life
And give you everything
You'll never want for nothing
I will give the world to you
I'll always be your queen
My love will never forsake you;
I love you
And with this ring I swear
To place no one above you
My heart is yours forever
To have and to hold
Never let go
I promise this day
Forever I'll stay, my love
The first time I saw you
I knew I'd make you mine
We'll be together
Loving each other for all time
Each day I wake up
I will have you by my side
The love I have for you
Grows deeper everyday
And each night before bed
I'll get on my knees and pray
Our love will always be strong

Bless this day with heaven's love
I love you
And with this ring I swear
To place no one above you
My heart is yours forever
To have and to hold
Never let go
I promise this day
Forever I'll stay, my love.

IV. Thoughts for Moments

How Are We Living

Look at how we're living
Is there something wrong with us
Lately it seems to be that
Some black folks are really mixed up
We have lost our focus
Need to get our priorities straight
Especially for the young ones
And the sake of our whole race;
Our love for our community
Has slowly been replaced
By a bitter animosity
Bordering of self-hate
Getting money is now
Our foremost concern
Chasing the American dream
But we often aren't willing
To be patient and work
To get the dollars for which we fen
We do some things to obtain
That paper immediately
Things that should disgust us;
When we look at the affect on our community
Some of us are standing on corners
All day every day
Selling poison to one another
To live in the fast lane
And others of us are shaking tail
Just to make a quick buck
Never stopping to think about
Other ways to change our luck
Many of us are toting arms
To take the life of another man
Quick to take his last breath
Over any little thing
And many of us are having babies

Children with no parents in sight
Growing up without any guidance
Having to find their own way in life;
And when some of us do come up
How do we spend our wealth
Rims and gold and platinum things
The trapping of uneducated success
We often fail to see
That there is a better way
Saving and investing in our community
Would help us see a better day
Many of our problems
We want to blame on the man
But maybe we need to examine ourselves
Are we doing all we can;
Created as kings and queens
We have deviated from our throne
Failing to understand our destiny
Is controlled by us alone
We need to open our eyes
Make the most of what we are given
Rise above the meaningless stuff
Examine how we are living.

Take A Chance

Take a chance
Break a mold
Go out on a limb
Pave your own road
A risk is often
Hard to take
Because of fear
That it's a mistake
But the greatest risks
Often have the greatest rewards
And if you don't take the chance
You'll get nothing for sure
So though the results aren't guaranteed
You'll have to take a chance
To ever succeed.

A Woman's Worth

Am I a whole woman
Or am I nothing without a man;
Does what I do matter
Or am I only as successful as my husband;
If I never get married
Is there something wrong with me
Will they say 'It's too bad she never settled down
Even though she has all those degrees;
What if I choose a carpenter
Am I not as good as a doctor's wife
She snagged the rich one
While my man is only working class;
If I choose to stay at home
Does the size of the home make me
Or does my worth depend on
The man beside me?

Fooling Yourself

Telling lies
All the time
You may begin
To believe your own
The stories you create
To impress others
May begin to
Take over your mind
Tricking others
To think of you better
You may believe
Their thoughts are justified
Being a fake
May erode your reality
Have you thinking
Your fraud is genuine
So when you write
A fictitious resume
Of everything you have done in life
Be careful not to take it to heart
Because others may
See through your lies
When you look around
You may just see
That your only fool is you.

Street Preachers

He who hath no sin
Shall cast the first stone
So instead of standing in judgment of others
Why don't you leave them alone;
You say they are wrong
They will go to hell
But if you keep throwing stones
This is where you will dwell;
There is only one Jesus
And no human is as great
So for all the street preachers
Born two-thousand years too late
Live and let live
Let God be the judge;
Because for each rock you throw
On your holy record goes a smudge;
Before you look at others
And talk about what they do
Take a good look at yourself
The sinner might be you.

What Goes Around

For every action there is supposed to be an equal reaction
Some cosmic justice to balance the scales;
Karma for all the things you have done
The people you have hurt, stepped on, done wrong;
So, I don't spend my time thinking of revenge
Because I know you will get yours in the end;
If what goes around really does come back around
What is in store for you is worse than any punishment I could have
found.

Get Up

When you fall down
Lose your footing in this world
Don't just lay there
With your face to the ground
Pull yourself together
With all the strength that you have
Get to your knees
And push yourself on
Get up off the ground;

In life we all will fall
Over a few stones in our path
But the ones who make it
To see a better day
Don't stay on the ground
With knees battered and bloodied
And your hands showing the cuts
You still have the power
To lift yourself back up.

V. God

Faith

Faith is believing in that which you cannot see
Trusting in that which you cannot touch
Knowing God is there though it cannot be proved
Not wavering in that belief, but holding true;

Faith will get us through some of our toughest times
Our darkest hours when all seems bleak
Having faith gives us the strength to go on
When the winds of adversity blow-in, it keeps us strong;

The origin of faith does not come from a scientific theory
There's no chemical formula to prove God's existence
Having faith is going out on a limb
And knowing that God has the strength of that limb
And it won't break beneath your feet.

Dance with the Devil

All around us
The devil does his dance
Enticing
Inviting
Exciting dark dance
Beckoning us to join in
His sinful two-step
The devil tries to wrap his arms around us
Engage in a slow dance
A sensual dance
The forbidden dance
A dance that takes our soul
And the weak minded
Unguided
Vulnerable
Enter the dance floor.

God's Love

Nothing compares to God's love
Not the love of a mother
A spouse or a friend
God's love is unconditional
He will never abandon you
God loves us on our good days
And even on our bad
God loves us everyday
In the mist of our mistakes
God's love is a rock
Strong and stable
A love that is always there
When you need love the most
God's love is deep
He's not a fair-weather friend
He will always love you
When you can't find another
The love of God is like the sun
To warn up a gloomy day
God's love is the greatest love
Just open up your heart
And let His love in.

Lord I Pray

Lord I pray
That you give me the strength
To make it through the day
And along with strength
You give me the wisdom
To live my life the right way
And please dear Lord
Make my faith solid
So that I know you're always there
And with my faith
Grant me determination
To pull me through
Moments of despair
Oh, and Lord I ask
That you teach me patience
But with others and myself
And God most importantly
Please keep me in good health
Lord I need love
And courage and compassion
All those things
To make me a better person
Lord I pray.

God Was There

God gives you struggles
To show you that you are strong
He puts you through trials
To teach you to move on;

He shows you your true character
At your weakest place
When you hit rock bottom
He lets you know what you can face;

Overcome, survive because you are tough
Not a fragile little girl anymore
He did all this for you
To show you what you could endure;

Only the strong survive
And He wanted you to see
That you're a survivor
As strong as anyone could be;

So the times when you cried at night
Thinking, if there is a God, then where?
Remember through all those dark hours
When God was there!

Hi God

Hi God, it's me
One of your many children
A lost sheep
Looking for guidance
So I turn to you
My father
My best friend
To help me
Guide me through
I won't ask you
Anything for me
Instead I pray for others
Help the world
Become a better place
Teach people to love each other
Show the child
Of a broken home
That crime is not the way
Tell the mother
Who can't feed her child
Tomorrow will be a bright day
Give the children
Something to live for
In a world where they can feel safe
If you do nothing more for me God;
All I ask is…
You hear my neighbor
When she kneels to pray.

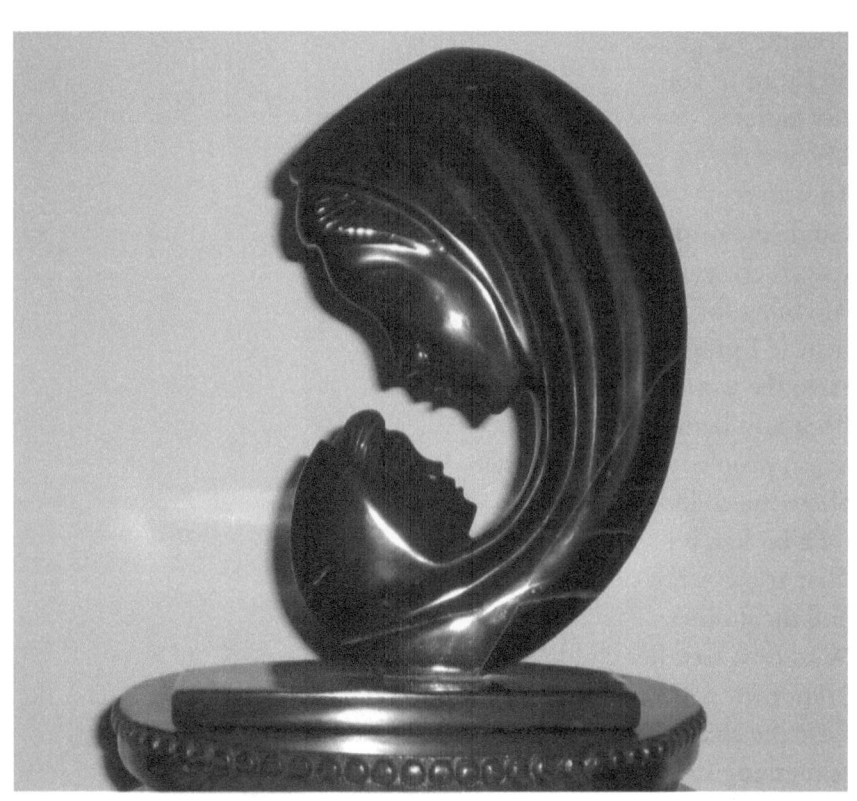

VI. Mothers, Strengthening the Family through Prayer

$\mathcal{T}$he third chapter of Genesis, verse 20, "And Adam called his wife's name Eve; because she was 'the Mother' of all living."

As we talk about, Mother's role in strengthening the family through prayer, it is important to understand:

Prayer is not a religious form without power. Prayer is effective and accurate and brings results, especially when you are praying God's Word!

When you pray according to the scriptures, you can be assured that you are praying in line with God's Will and that He will honor His Word.

There are many issues facing today's mothers and the demand for your time maybe overwhelming but you must keep your prayer appointment with God. Developing an effectual prayer life and consistently reading the Bible enables you to become more intimately acquainted with God. You learn to recognize and understand His nature, and appreciate the value He has placed on you.

The God Who created woman is the Lord, Who gives the word of power. He calls women to bear and publish the good news, and we are a great host. (Psalm 68:11)

Remember, God created human to be like Himself; He made men and women (Genesis 1:26);

So, mothers –
What were God's intentions when He designed woman?
Did God give equal power and ability to both woman and man?
What do you believe about the woman in Proverb 31?

I have concluded that she is a composite of God's woman describing various gifts and talents deposited within the makeup of individuals. God created you a distinctive person and to find the answers to these questions ---the Holy Spirit is the One who will guide you into all Truth – the Reality of who you are.

So, how do mothers strengthen the family through prayer?

First, find a quiet, peaceful space, and set aside time, preferably at the beginning of your day to commune with God. Begin by addressing Him as "Our Father". Acknowledge His Sovereignty asking Him to hallow His Name in your personality, and in all your roles and activities. Make your petitions known to Him, forgiving others as freely as He has forgiven you. Affirm the Lordship of Jesus and submit to the constant ministry of transformation by the Holy Spirit.

Remember, Prayer is conversation with our Heavenly Father. Take time to talk to Him and listen for His quiet, gentle voice. He knows your present circumstances and your future, and has already provided exactly what you need for the day.

Mothers, as you pray you will be enforcing the prayer armor mothers have been instructed to put on in Ephesians 6:11. The fabric from which the armor is made is the Word of God.

We are to live by every word that proceeds from the mouth of God. We desire the whole counsel of God, because we know it changes. By receiving that counsel, Mothers you will be transformed (changed) by the entire renewal of your mind – by its new ideals and its new attitude – so that you may prove, for yourself, what is good and acceptable and perfect Will of God, even the thing which is good and acceptable and perfect in His sight for you (Rom.12:2).

So often it is asked, how many time should I pray the same prayer?

The answer is simple: you pray until you know the answer is fixed in your heart. After that, you need to repeat the prayer whenever adverse circumstances or long delays cause you to be tempted to doubt that your prayer has been heard and your request granted.

The Word of God is your weapon against the temptation to lose heart and grow weary in your prayer life. When that word of promise becomes fixed in your heart, you will find yourself praising, giving glory to God for the answer, even when the only evidence you have is your faith.

But, remember you are the righteousness of God in Christ, and your prayers will avail much. They will bring salvation to the sinner, deliverance to the oppressed, healing to the sick and prosperity to the poor.

Thus, we are to pray at all times- on every occasion, in season and out of season, in the Spirit, with all manner of prayer (Eph. 6:18).

Pray for personal needs and strength – walking in humility; health and healing; peaceful sleep. It is God's desire that you know His Will for your life;

Pray, stand in the gap for others – sons, daughters, husbands, fathers, other family members, friends, co-workers, and acquaintances, those whom you do not know;

Pray for ministry – salvation of the lost; vision for the Church and hope of Peace for the Nation;

Your prayers will usher in the next move of God on the earth.

But, there is something to think about, prayer does not cause faith to work, it is faith, which causes prayer to work. Therefore, any prayer problem is a problem of doubt – doubting the integrity of the Word and the ability of God to stand behind His promises.

We can spend fruitless hours in prayer if our hearts are not prepared beforehand. Preparation of the heart, the spirit comes from meditation on who we are in Christ, what He is to us, and what the Holy Spirit can mean to us. As God told Joshua (Josh. 1:8), as we mediate on the

Word day and night, and do according to all that is written, then shall we make our way prosperous and have good success.

My prayer is that you will find strength, comfort, courage, and fortitude as you pray according to God's Word. Grow in grace and the knowledge of our Lord and Savior, ever learning, ever growing, and ever achieving.

Faith comes by hearing, and hearing by the Word. When you hear yourself pray you will discover that you truly believe. God is a rewarder of those who believe that He is.

Mothers remember, in the very process of praying, your life will be changed as you go from faith to faith and from glory to glory.

God did not leave us here without His thoughts and His ways, for we have His Word –His bond. God instructs us to call Him, and He will answer and show us great and mighty things for our families.

Just pray!